T0020809

PIANO
Adventures® *by Nancy and Randall Faber*
THE BASIC PIANO METHOD

_____ is sightreading this book!
(your name)

Production Coordinator: Jon Ophoff
Cover: Terpstra Design, San Francisco
Illustrations: Erika LeBarre

ISBN 978-1-61677-637-4

CHART YOUR PROGRESS

SIGHTREADING SKILL

Good sightreading skill is a powerful asset for the developing musician. It makes every step of music-making easier. With the right tools and a little work, sightreading skill can be developed to great benefit.

This book builds confident readers in two ways: 1) recognition of individual notes, and 2) perception of note patterns, both rhythmic and melodic.

In language literacy, the reader must not only identify single words, but also group words together for understanding. Similarly, music reading involves more than note naming. The sightreader tracks horizontally and vertically, observing intervals and contour while gleaning familiar patterns that make up the musical context.

This decoding skill requires repetition within familiar musical contexts. In other words, pattern recognition develops by seeing a lot of the same patterns. Accordingly, this book presents musical variations to sharpen perception of the new against a backdrop of the familiar. To use the literacy analogy, the musician must not only identify single notes, but also group notes into musical patterns for understanding.

How to Use

This book is organized into sets of 5 exercises, for 5 days of practice. Each set provides variations on a piece from the **Piano Adventures® Level 1 Lesson Book (2nd Edition).** Play one exercise a day, completing one set per week.

Though the student is not required to repeatedly "practice" the sightreading exercise, each should be repeated once or twice as indicated by the repeat sign. For an extra workout, play each of the previous exercises in the set before playing the new exercise of the day.

Curiosity and Fun

The "Don't Practice This!" motto is a bold statement which has an obvious psychological impact. It reminds us that sightreading is indeed "the first time through" and it reminds us to keep the activity fun.

The comic-style illustrations (educational art) draw students through consecutive pages by stimulating curiosity. Little Treble, Little Bass, Penny Piano, Freddie Forte, Buddy Barline and other characters captivate the beginning reader with musical questions, antics and requests. Each page presents a new "learning vignette" in a spirit of fun.

Level of Difficulty

It is most beneficial to sightread at the appropriate level of difficulty. Some experts say that a child should not stumble on more than three or four words per page when learning to read. Similarly, a sightreader should not stumble on more than three or four notes per page. This Piano Adventures® Sightreading Book is carefully written to match the Level 1 difficulty and to provide appropriate challenge.

Marking Progress

Students are encouraged to draw a large **X** over each completed exercise. This instruction is so out of the ordinary that students find it immensely satisfying to mark their progress in this way.

Additionally, students wishing to celebrate the completion of a set may color the illustration of Day 5.

Some students may exclaim about the thickness of the book! They soon are rewarded to find how fast they can move through it. Indeed, with confidence increasing, the student can take pride in moving to completion of this very large book...and do so with a crescendo of achievement.

DON'T PRACTICE THIS!

Instructions to Student

1. Scan the music before playing.

2. Play the music without stopping.

Always repeat, then cross it out.

3. Play one exercise a day.

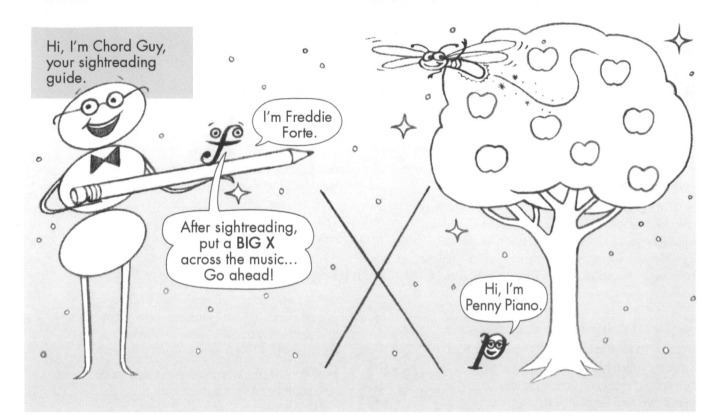

DAY 1: Firefly

Count: "1-2-3-4, 1-2-Ready-Play"

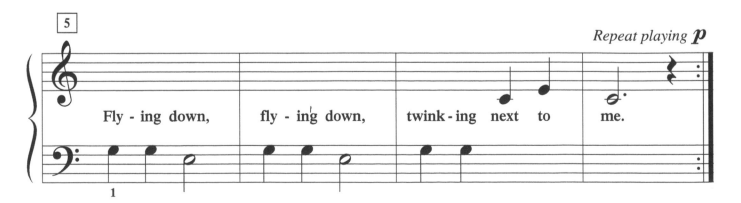

DAY 2: Firefly

What does *mf* mean?

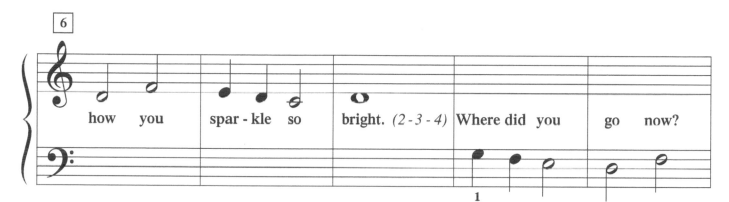

Put a ✓ above each measure with a **skip**. How many skips are there?

I see 6!

I see 8!

WHO IS RIGHT? LITTLE TREBLE OR LITTLE BASS (circle one)

7

DAY 3: Firefly

Does each measure step or skip?

DAY 4: Firefly

Does each measure step or skip?

DAY 5: Firefly

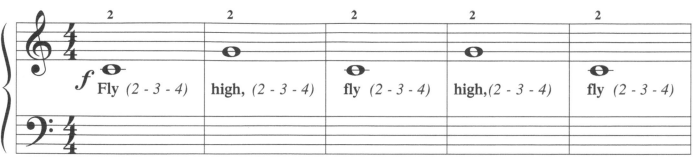

DON'T PRACTICE THIS!

Use only finger 2's to play DAY 5. You will need to lift your hand from one key to the next.

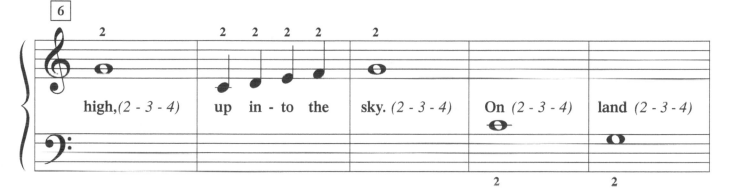

Hold the damper pedal down throughout.

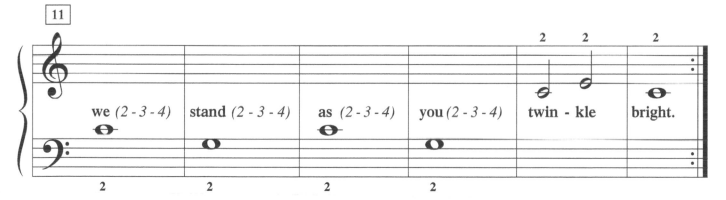

WOW! You made it to **DAY 5**! The Quarter Note Guys applaud you!

Way to go Sightreader!!!!!

DAY 1: Sailing in the Sun

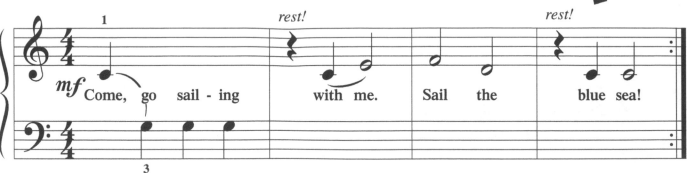

DAY 2: Sailing in the Sun

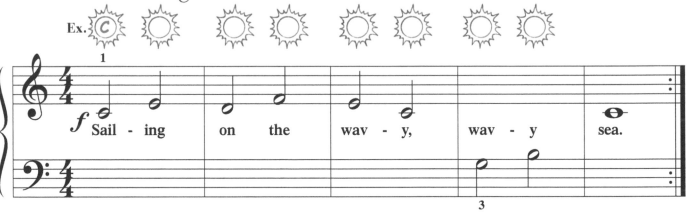

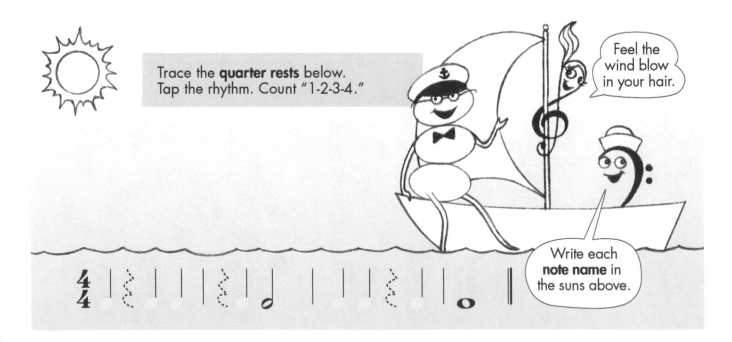

Pattern 1

Pattern 2

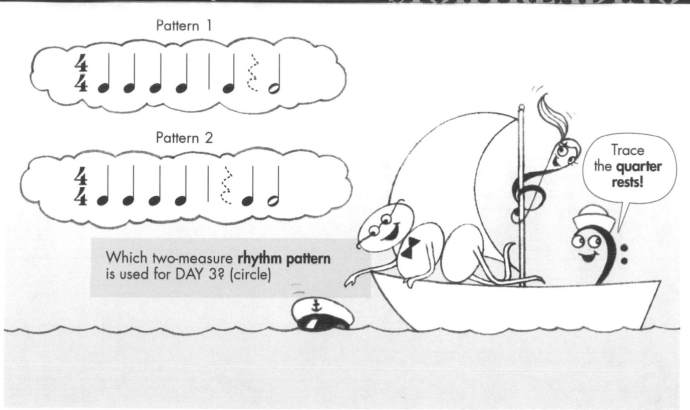

Which two-measure **rhythm pattern** is used for DAY 3? (circle)

Trace the **quarter rests!**

DAY 3: Sailing in the Sun

DON'T PRACTICE THIS!

Sail-boat rac - es   *rest!* are fun,   in the wind and   the sun.

We'll go soar-ing   so free   out up - on the   blue sea.

DAY 4: Sailing in the Sun

DON'T PRACTICE THIS!

mf Come with me and *rest!* we'll float in my lit - tle sail-boat.

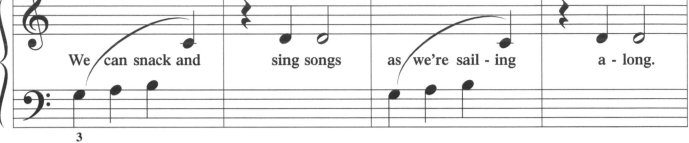

We can snack and sing songs as we're sail - ing a - long.

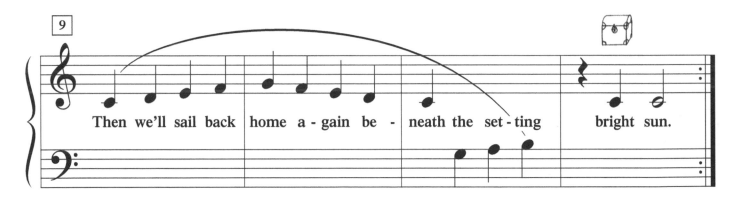

Then we'll sail back home a - gain be - neath the set - ting bright sun.

Write the note names in the treasure chests above. Arrrr!

Shriek!

It's a pirate ship!

Ahoy!

DAY 5: Sailing in the Sun

Use only 2's to play this song.

DON'T PRACTICE THIS!

DAY 1: The Haunted Mouse

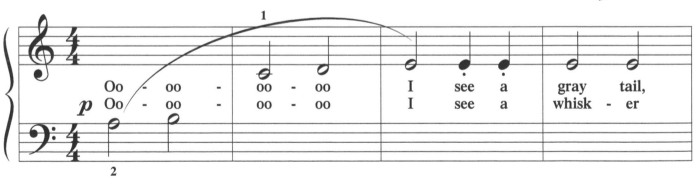

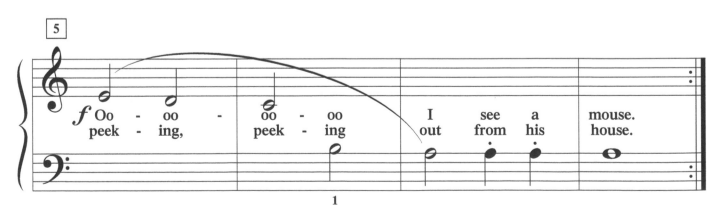

14

DAY 2: The Haunted Mouse

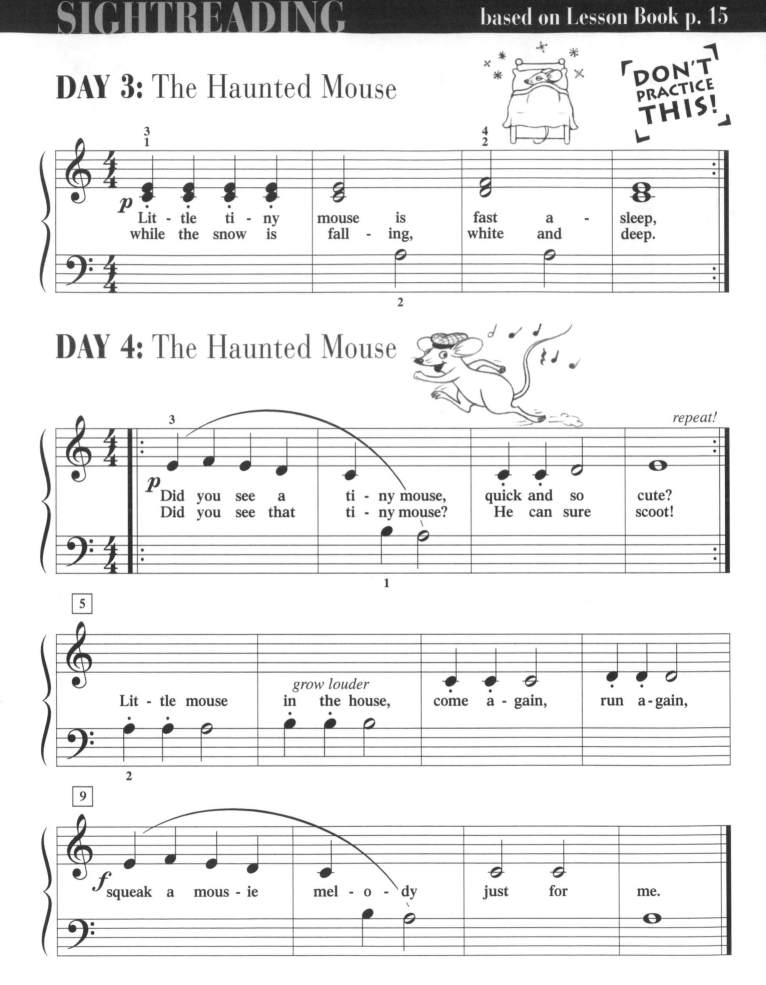

DAY 3: The Haunted Mouse

DON'T PRACTICE THIS!

p Lit - tle ti - ny mouse is fast a - sleep,
while the snow is fall - ing, white and deep.

DAY 4: The Haunted Mouse

repeat!

p Did you see a ti - ny mouse, quick and so cute?
Did you see that ti - ny mouse? He can sure scoot!

5

Lit - tle mouse   *grow louder* in the house, come a - gain, run a - gain,

9

f squeak a mous - ie mel - o - dy just for me.

DAY 5: The Haunted Mouse

Use only finger 2's to play this song.

DON'T PRACTICE THIS!

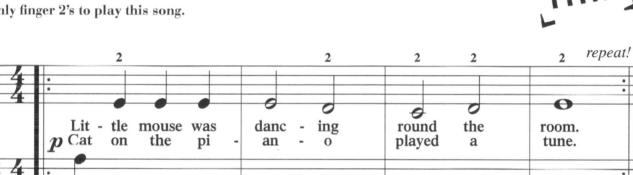

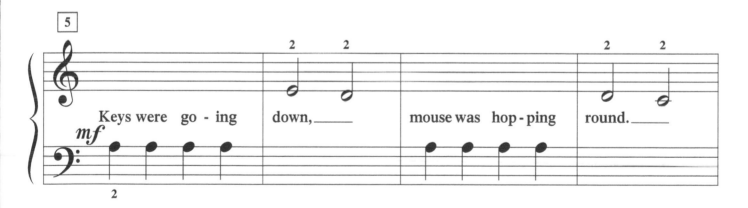

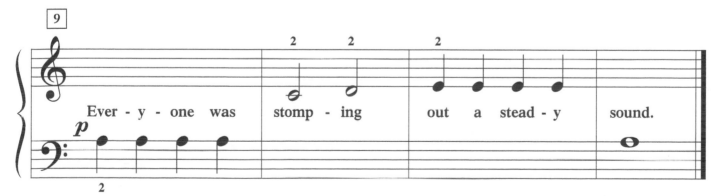

17

Put an X through each INCORRECT measure in 3/4 time.

Hi, I'm Buddy Barline. May I have this dance?

1-2-3, 1-2-3

DAY 1: Classic Dance

DON'T PRACTICE THIS!

Count: "1-2-3, Read-y Play"

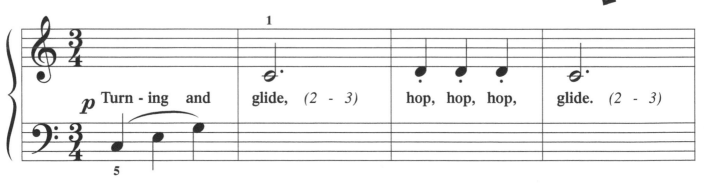

p Turn - ing and | glide, *(2 - 3)* | hop, hop, hop, | glide. *(2 - 3)*

mf Hop, hop, hop, | glid - ing then | hop back to | C. *(2 - 3)*

DAY 2: Classic Dance

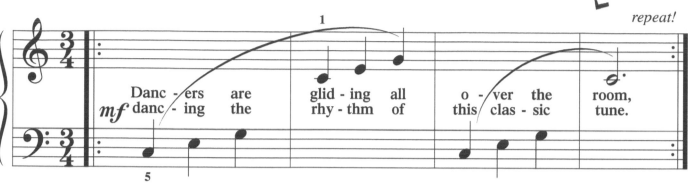

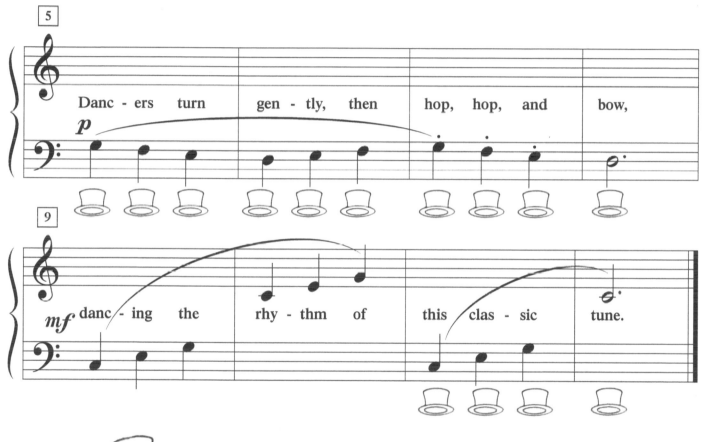

Write the **note name** in each hat above.

1-2-3, 1-2-3

Watch me twirl!

DAY 3: Classic Dance

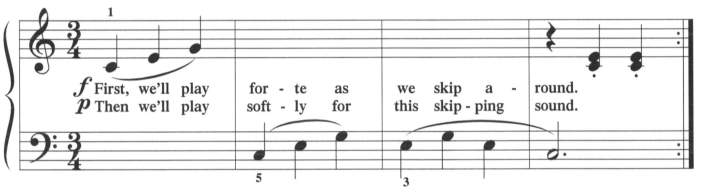

f First, we'll play   for - te   as   we   skip a - round.
p Then we'll play   soft - ly   for   this skip - ping   sound.

DAY 4: Classic Dance

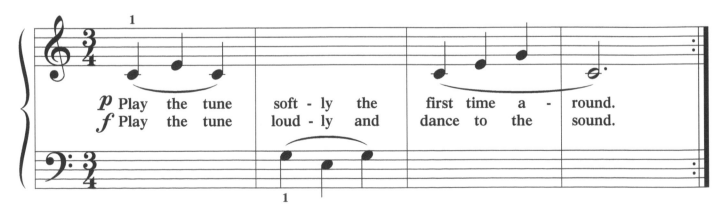

p Play   the   tune   soft - ly   the   first time a - round.
f Play   the   tune   loud - ly   and   dance   to   the   sound.

DAY 5: Classic Dance

Use only finger 2's to play this song.

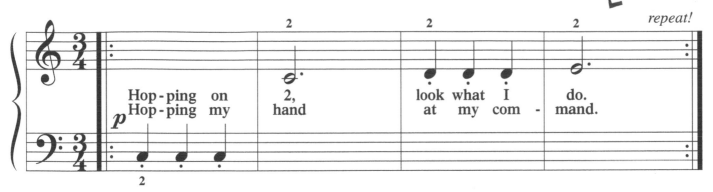

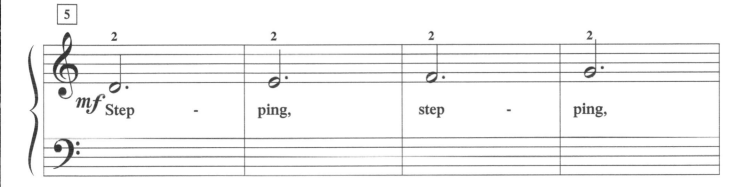

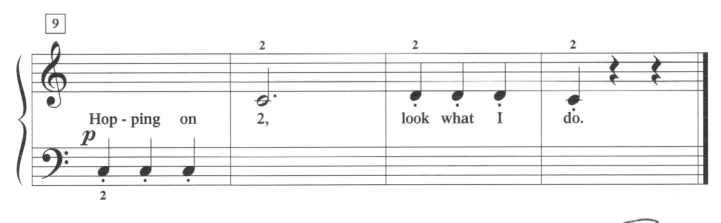

DAY 1: Half-Time Show

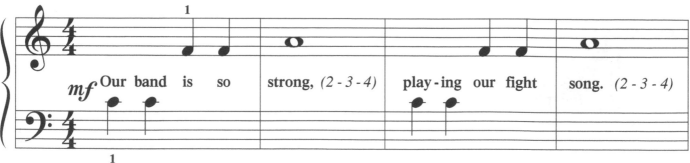

mf Our band is so | strong, *(2 - 3 - 4)* | play-ing our fight | song. *(2 - 3 - 4)*

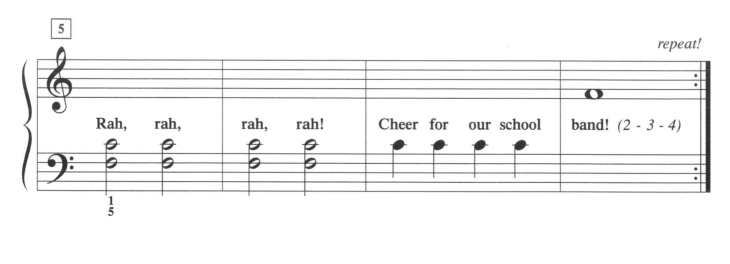

repeat!

Rah, rah, | rah, rah! | Cheer for our school | band! *(2 - 3 - 4)*

Draw **bar lines** to complete the rhythm above.

Look, Mouse is the drum major!

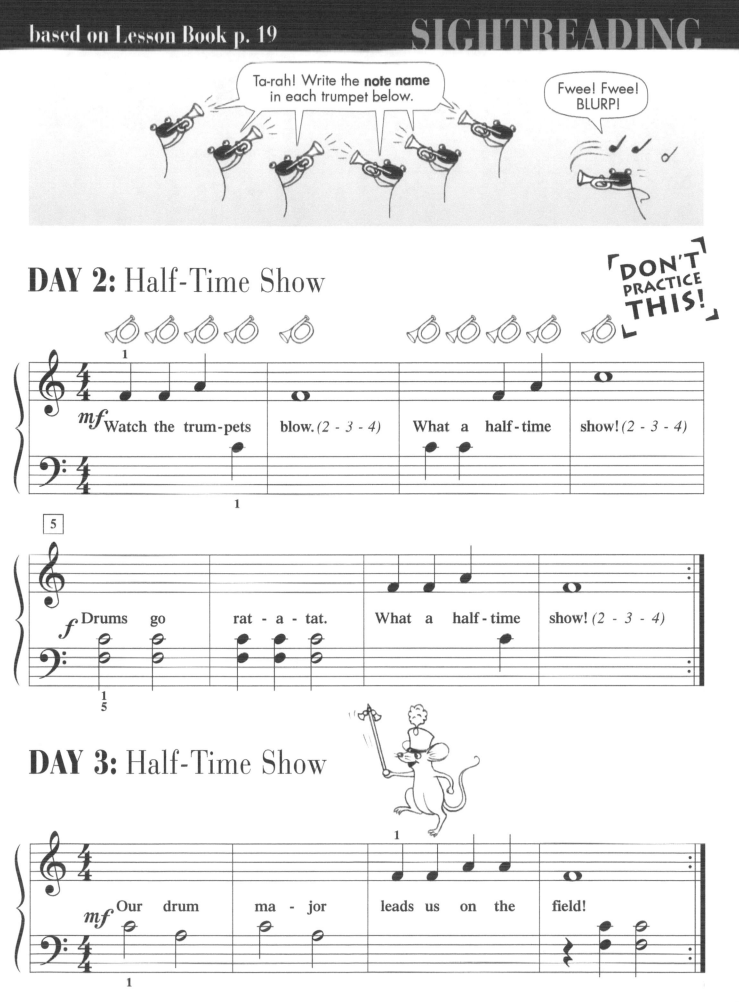

DAY 2: Half-Time Show

DAY 3: Half-Time Show

DAY 4: Half-Time Show

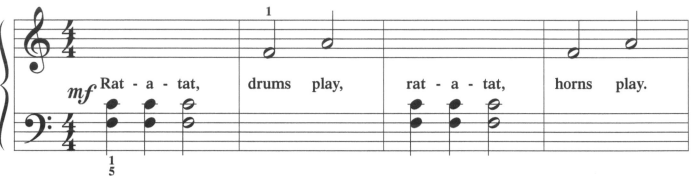

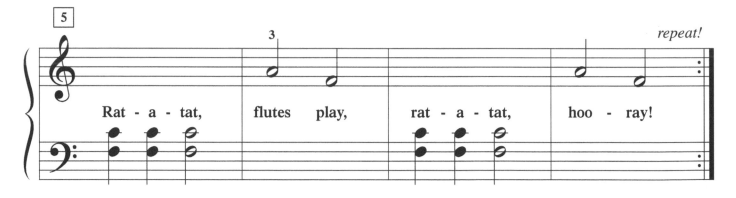

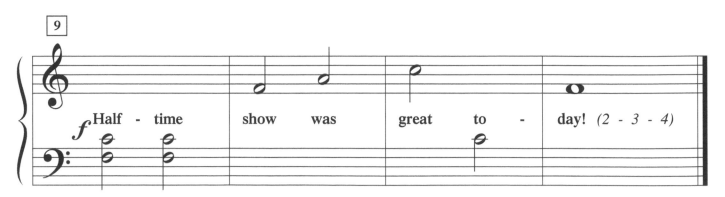

DAY 5: Half-Time Show

DON'T
PRACTICE
THIS!

Use only finger 2's to play this song. Hold the damper pedal if you wish.

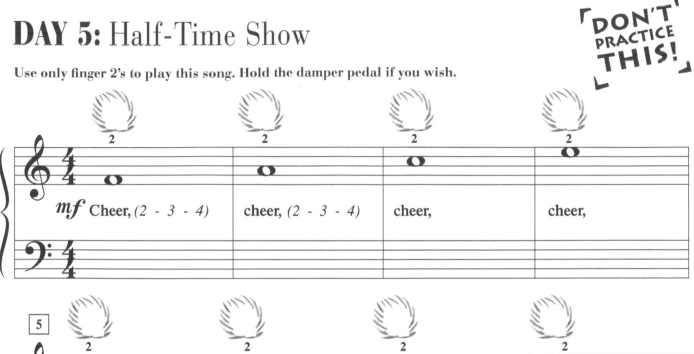

mf Cheer, *(2 - 3 - 4)*   cheer, *(2 - 3 - 4)*   cheer,   cheer,

5

cheer,   cheer,   cheer,   cheer.

9

f Look, here comes the   band. *(2 - 3 - 4)*   Let's   all   stand. *(2 - 3 - 4)*

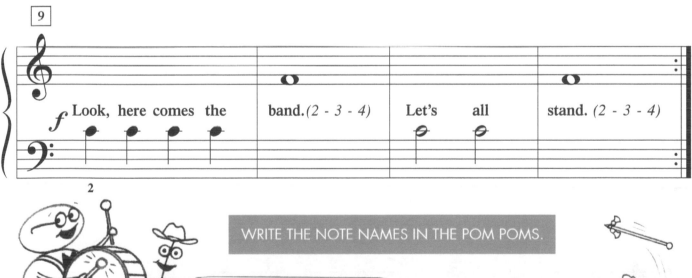

WRITE THE NOTE NAMES IN THE POM POMS.

DAY 5! We're cheering for you, Sightreader!

DAY 1: Li'l Liza Jane

DON'T PRACTICE THIS!

Lit - tle Li - za | Jane lives | next door to | me.
I can hear her | prac - tice | next door to | me.

DAY 2: Li'l Liza Jane

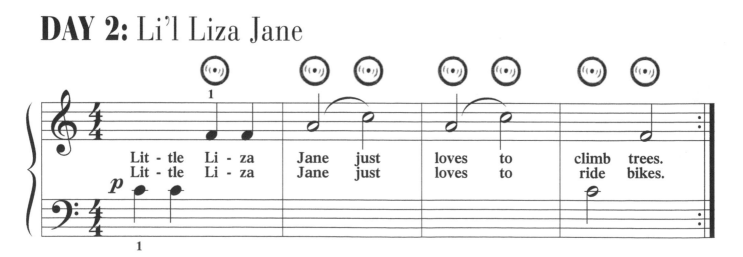

Lit - tle Li - za | Jane just | loves to | climb trees.
Lit - tle Li - za | Jane just just | loves to | ride bikes.

SIGHTREADING

DAY 3: Li'l Liza Jane

Come on out, let's shoot some bas - ket - balls.

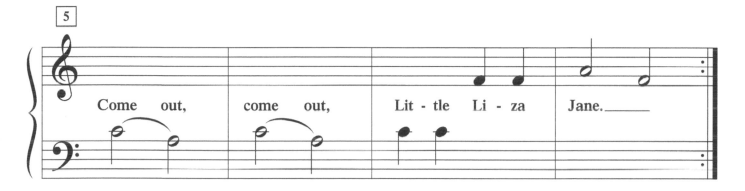

Come out, come out, Lit - tle Li - za Jane.____

Put a ✓ above each measure with a **skip**. How many measures have a skip?

I see 4 measures.

I see 6 measures.

I see 3 measures.

WHO IS RIGHT? (circle one)

DAY 4: Li'l Liza Jane

DON'T PRACTICE THIS!

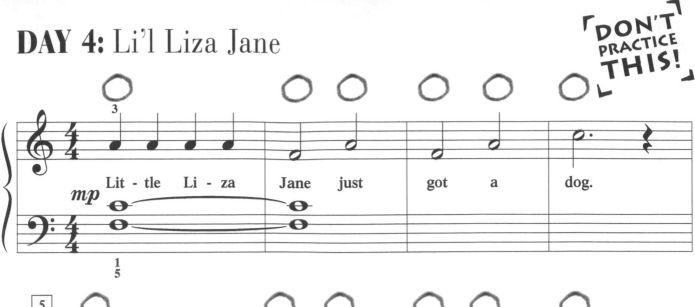

Lit - tle Li - za | Jane just | got a | dog.

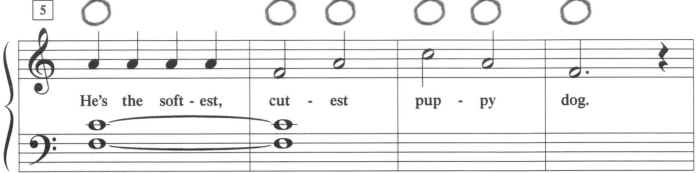

He's the soft - est, | cut - est | pup - py | dog.

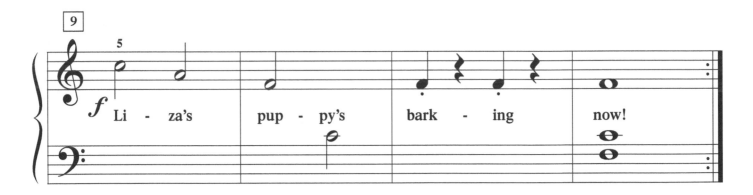

Li - za's | pup - py's | bark - ing | now!

Write the **note name** in each ball above.

NAME LIZA'S DOG _____

quarter note   half note   dotted half note   whole note

BIG congratulations!

DAY 5! Great job! Draw the **correct note** in each cloud.

DAY 5: Li'l Liza Jane

DON'T PRACTICE THIS!

Use only finger 2's to play the song.
Press the damper pedal if you wish!

f Lit - tle   Li - za   jumps and   skips

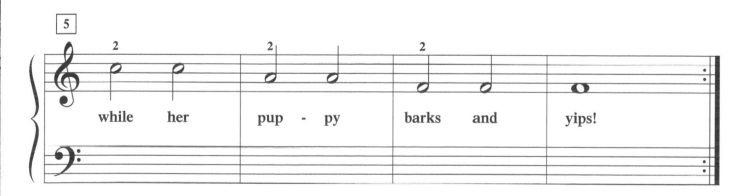

while her   pup - py   barks and   yips!

DAY 1: Mozart's Five Names

DON'T PRACTICE THIS!

Notice the R.H. shifts up to Treble C at measure 5.

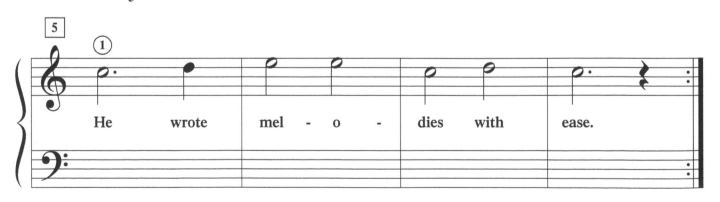

DAY 2: Mozart's Five Names

Notice the R.H. shifts up to Treble C at measure 5.

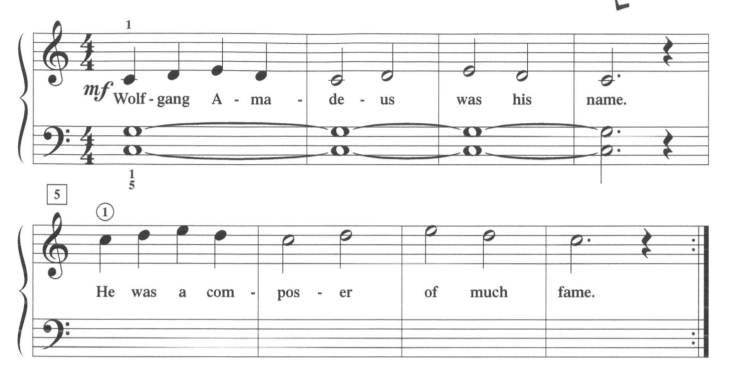

Wolf - gang A - ma - de - us was his name.

He was a com - pos - er of much fame.

DAY 3: Mozart's Five Names

Notice the R.H. shift at measure 3.

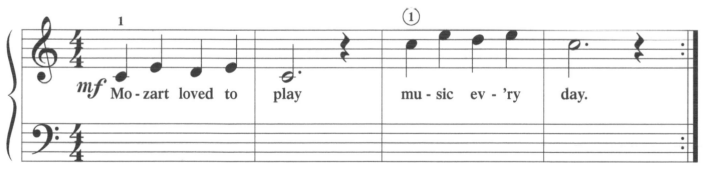

Mo - zart loved to play mu - sic ev - 'ry day.

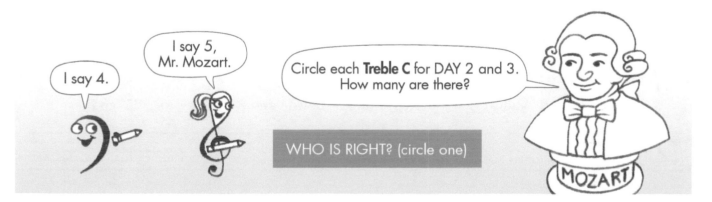

I say 4.

I say 5, Mr. Mozart.

Circle each **Treble C** for DAY 2 and 3. How many are there?

WHO IS RIGHT? (circle one)

MOZART

DAY 4: Mozart's Five Names

Spot the R.H. shift before you sightread.

DON'T PRACTICE THIS!

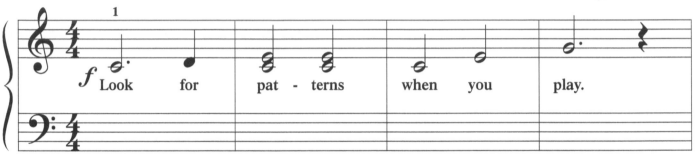

f Look for pat - terns when you play.

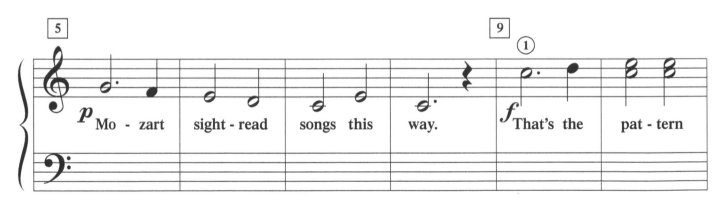

p Mo - zart sight - read songs this way. *f* That's the pat - tern

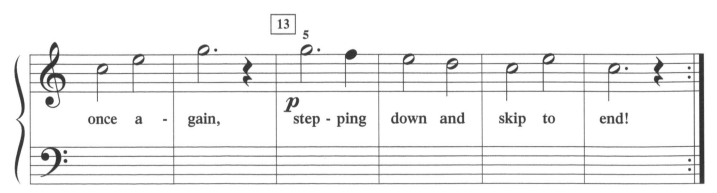

once a - gain, *p* step - ping down and skip to end!

SIGHTREADING

DAY 5: Mozart's Five Names

DON'T PRACTICE THIS!

Use only R.H. finger 2 to play this song.

mf This is a pat - tern, this is a pat - tern.

Sight-read notes, sight-read notes, up and down. *(2 - 3 - 4)*

p Now the pat-tern chang-es and steps up and down. *(2 - 3 - 4)*

DAY 5, Sightreader! Congratulations! Keep up the fine work.

MOZART

Write the **note names** in the wigs above.

Name the **treble space notes** that I tossed on the staff.

DAY 1: The Juggler

DON'T PRACTICE THIS!

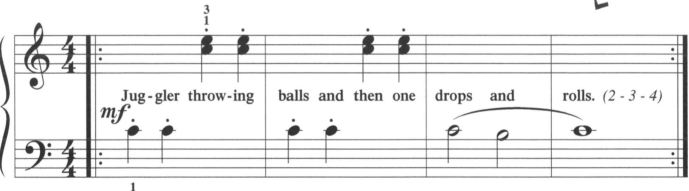

mf Jug-gler throw-ing | balls and then one | drops and | rolls. *(2 - 3 - 4)*

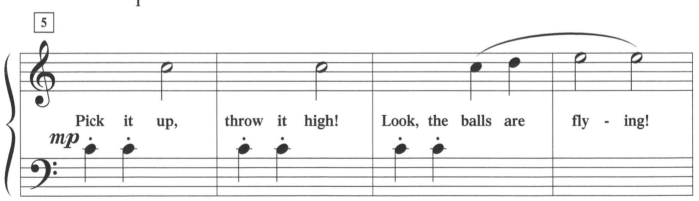

mp Pick it up, | throw it high! | Look, the balls are | fly - ing!

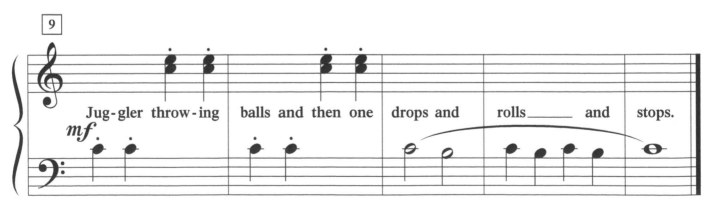

mf Jug-gler throw-ing | balls and then one | drops and | rolls_____ and | stops.

DAY 2: The Juggler

DON'T
PRACTICE
THIS!

First, I toss three or - ang - es, then I catch them one by one.
Next, I toss six or - ang - es. Jug - gling fruit is so much fun.

DAY 3: The Juggler

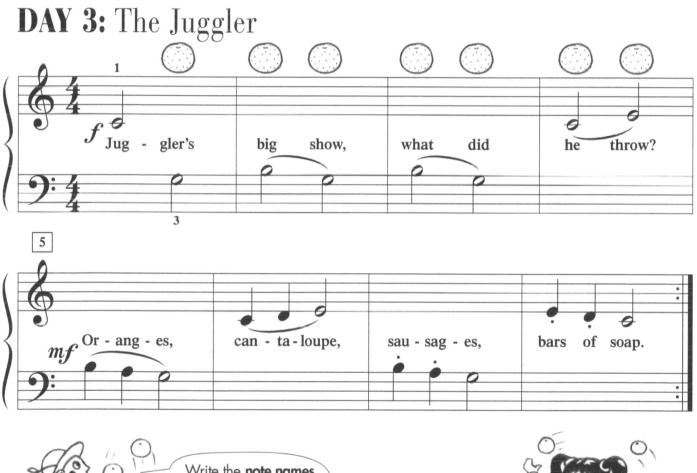

f Jug - gler's big show, what did he throw?

5

mf Or - ang - es, can - ta - loupe, sau - sag - es, bars of soap.

Write the **note names** in the oranges above.

Hey!

DAY 4: The Juggler

Write the **note name** in each apple!

SIGHTREADING

DAY 5: The Juggler

Use only finger 2's to play this song.

DON'T PRACTICE THIS!

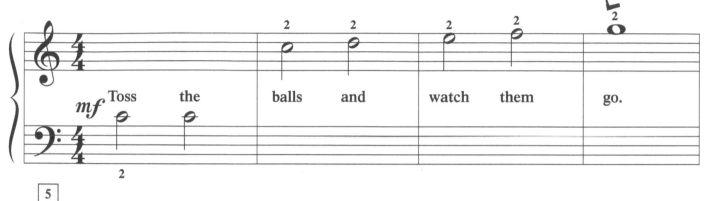

Toss the balls and watch them go.

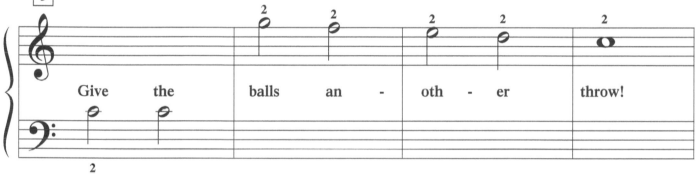

Give the balls an - oth - er throw!

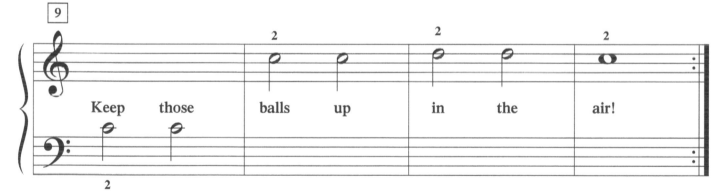

Keep those balls up in the air!

DAY 5!

Hooray for you!

Bravo. Woof!

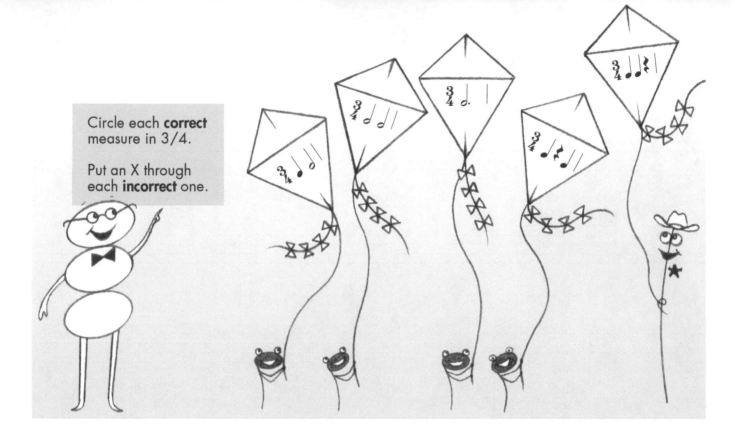

Circle each **correct** measure in 3/4.

Put an X through each **incorrect** one.

DAY 1: Kites in the Sky

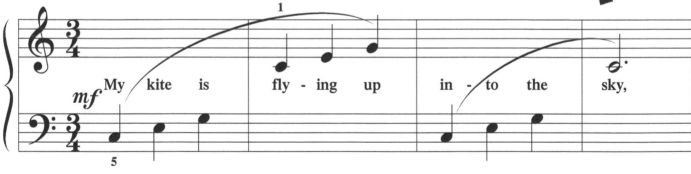

My kite is fly - ing up in - to the sky,

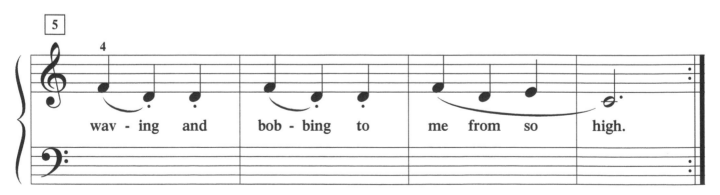

wav - ing and bob - bing to me from so high.

SIGHTREADING

DAY 2: Kites in the Sky

Circ - ling a - round, dip - ping.

Circ - ling a - round, dip - ping.

Circ - ling a - round, circ - ling a - round,

no wind to - day. Land - ing.

Write the **note names** in the kites above!

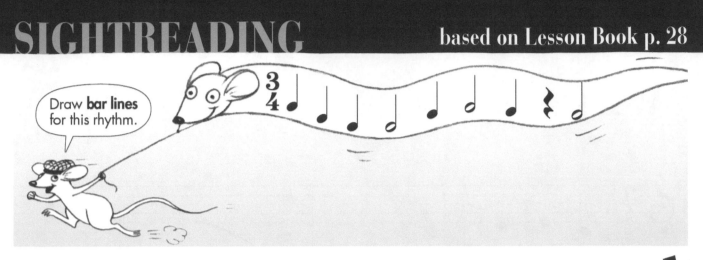

DAY 3: Kites in the Sky

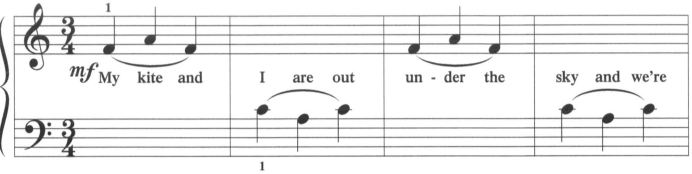

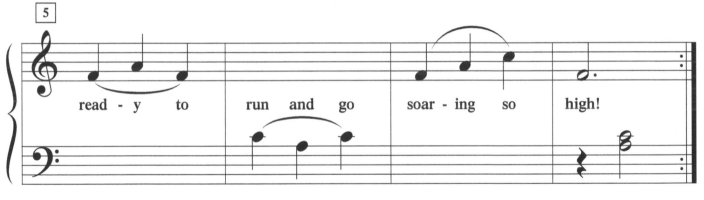

DAY 4: Kites in the Sky

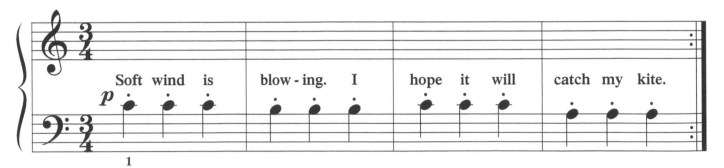

DAY 5: Kites in the Sky

Use only finger 2's to play this song.

DON'T PRACTICE THIS!

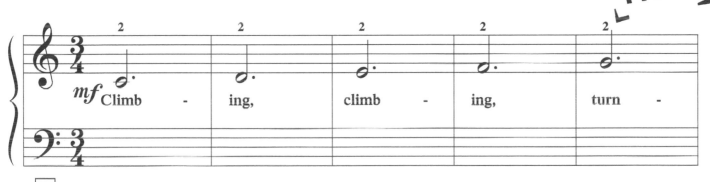

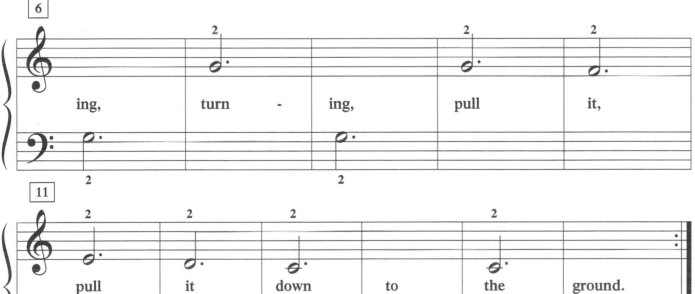

DAY 1: A Mixed-Up Song

Find the starting L.H. note before you begin.

DON'T PRACTICE THIS!

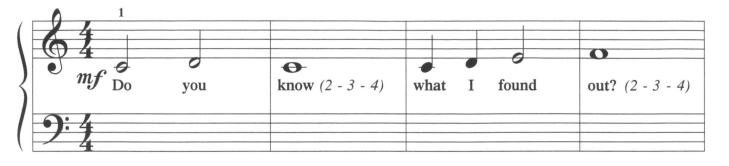

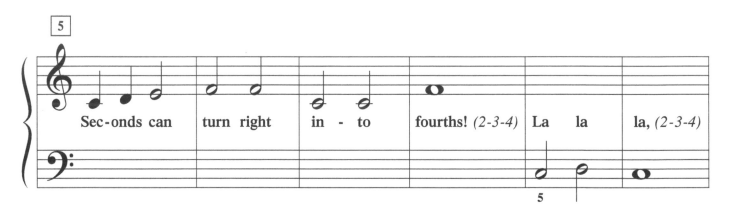

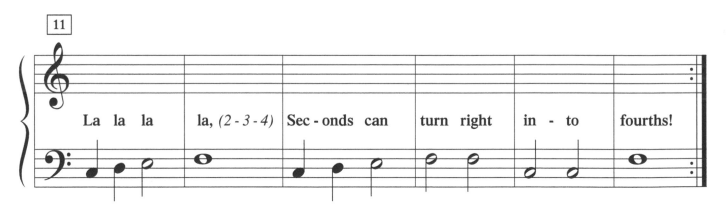

DAY 2: A Mixed-Up Song

Write the **note names** in the little blackboards.

DAY 3: A Mixed-Up Song

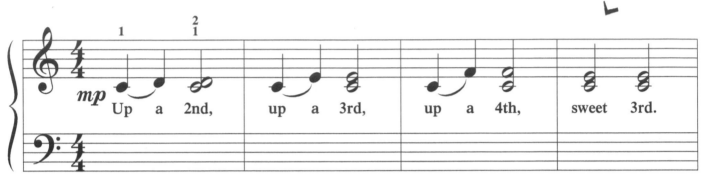

DAY 4: A Mixed-Up Song

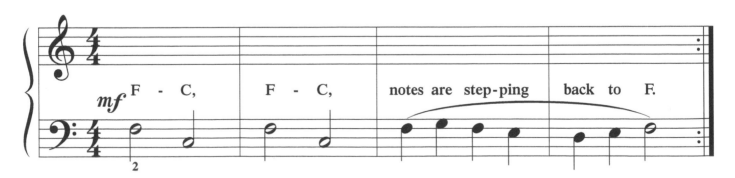

DAY 5: A Mixed-Up Song

┌ DON'T
PRACTICE
THIS! ┐

Hold the damper pedal down throughout the song.

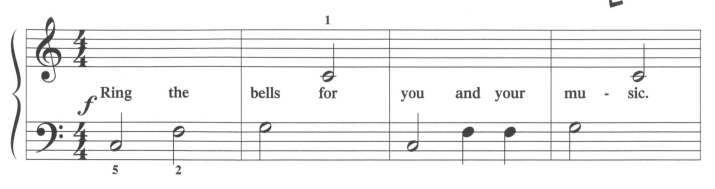

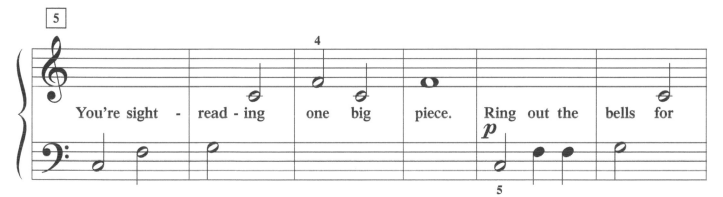

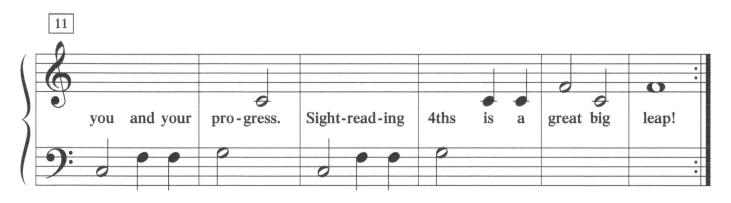

DAY 5! Well done! Write the correct letter name in each bell to show **4ths going up** the keyboard.

DAY 1: Runaway Rabbit

Do you begin on Middle C or Treble C?

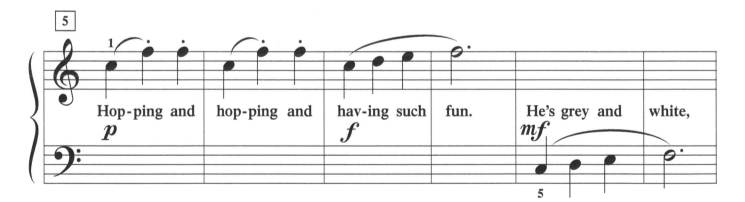

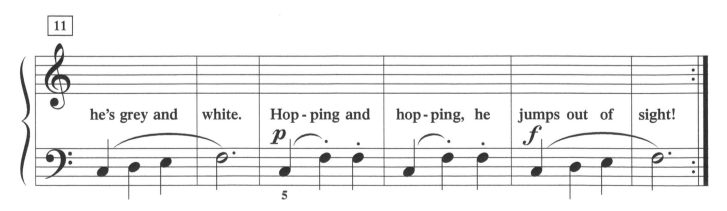

DAY 2: Runaway Rabbit

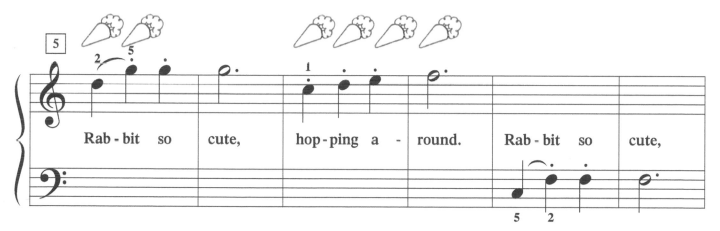

DAY 3: Runaway Rabbit

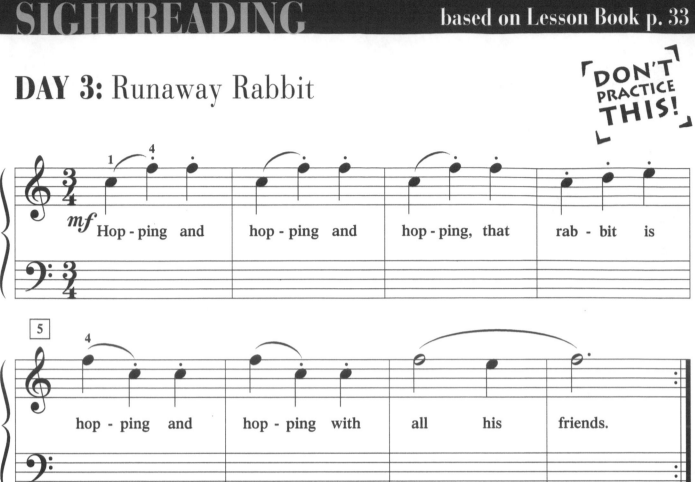

Hop - ping and hop - ping and hop - ping, that rab - bit is
hop - ping and hop - ping with all his friends.

DAY 4: Runaway Rabbit

Rab - bit, rab - bit, where are you go - ing?
Rab - bit, run home. Look how it's snow - ing!

How do you do, Mouse? Tell me. Does each tune above end on a **2nd** or a **4th**?

How do you do, Rabbit? I do not know this answer... for I am only a mouse.

HELP THE MOUSE. 2ND OR 4TH? (circle one)

DAY 5: Runaway Rabbit

Use only R.H. finger 2 to play this song.

p Hop, (rest, rest)　hop, hop, hop,　hop,　stop!

Hop, hop, hop,　stop!　Hop, hop, hop,　stop!

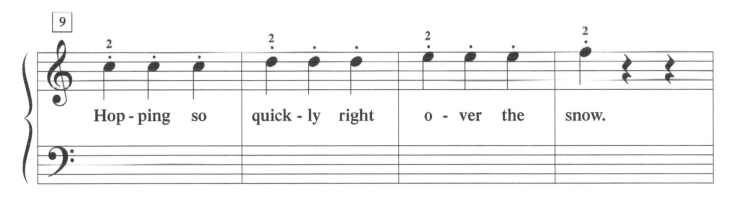

Hop - ping　so　quick - ly　right　o - ver the　snow.

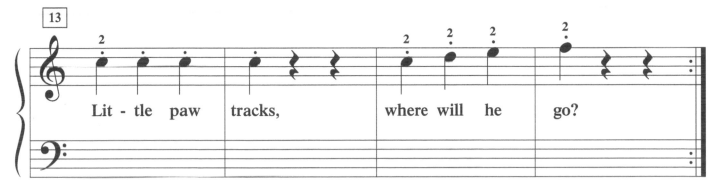

Lit - tle paw　tracks,　where will he　go?

CONGRATULATIONS! Signed, Runaway RABBIT

DAY 1: Lightly Row

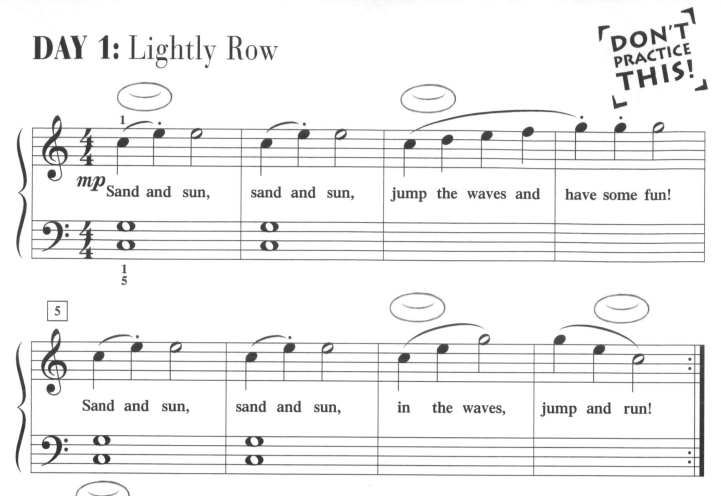

DAY 4: Lightly Row

DON'T PRACTICE THIS!

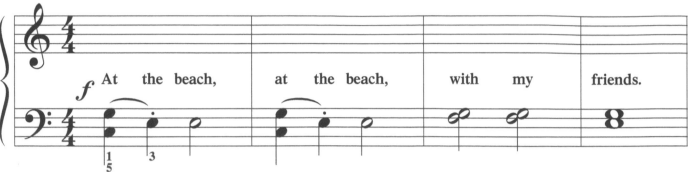

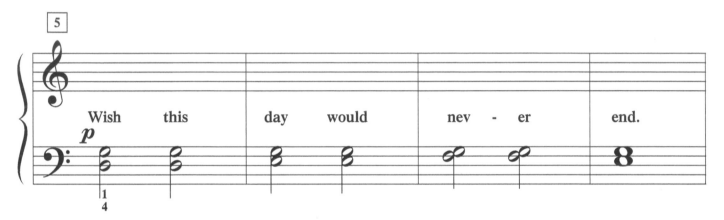

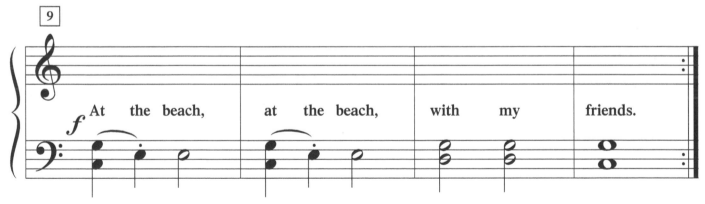

How many **5ths** are above?

Easy, 4!

5?

I say 3. Squeak!

WHO IS RIGHT? (circle one)

SIGHTREADING

DAY 5: Lightly Row

DON'T PRACTICE THIS!

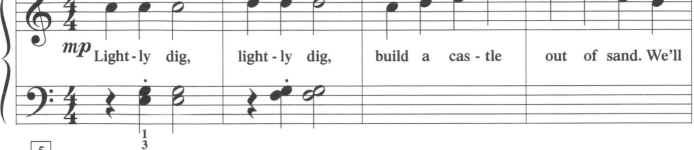

mp Light-ly dig, light-ly dig, build a cas-tle out of sand. We'll

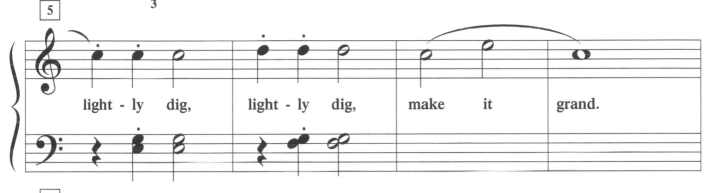

5

light-ly dig, light-ly dig, make it grand.

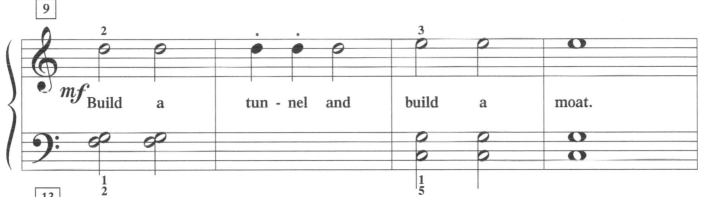

9

mf Build a tun-nel and build a moat.

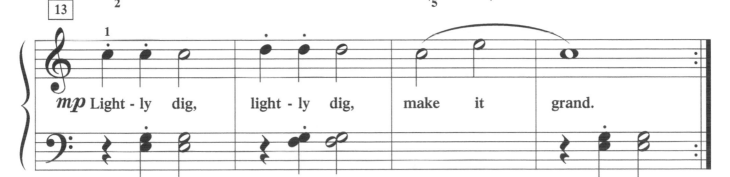

13

mp Light-ly dig, light-ly dig, make it grand.

CONGRATULATIONS...FOR DIGGING INTO SIGHTREADING.

DAY 1: Forest Drums

DON'T
PRACTICE
THIS!

Notice the starting position for each hand.

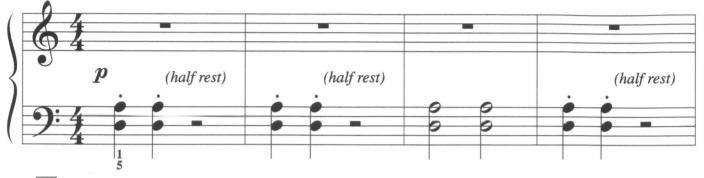

p (half rest) (half rest) (half rest)

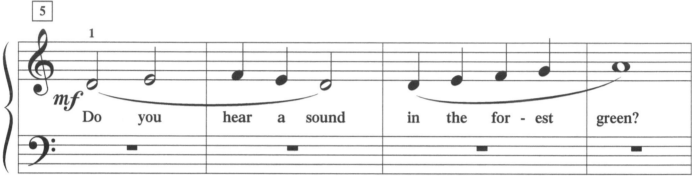

mf Do you hear a sound in the for - est green?

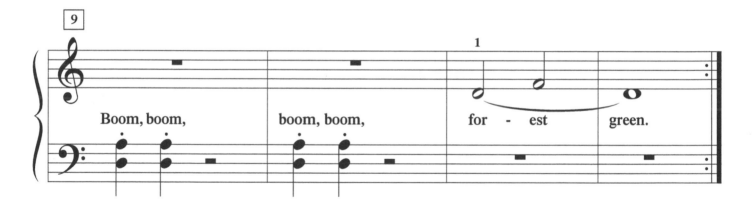

Boom, boom, boom, boom, for - est green.

Draw a **half** or **whole rest** on each forest drum.

half rest   whole rest   half rest

Write **1 2 3 4** for this rhythm.

DAY 2: Forest Drums

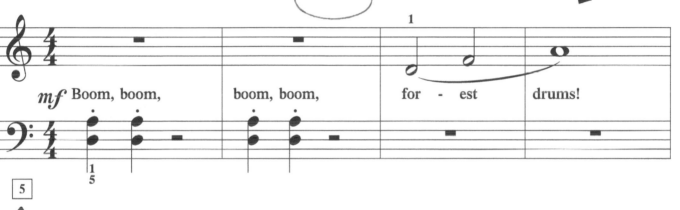

DON'T PRACTICE THIS!

mf Boom, boom, boom, boom, for - est drums!

Boom, boom, boom, boom, hear the for - est drums.

DAY 3: Forest Drums

f Do you see the for - est drums?
Can you hear the for - est drums?

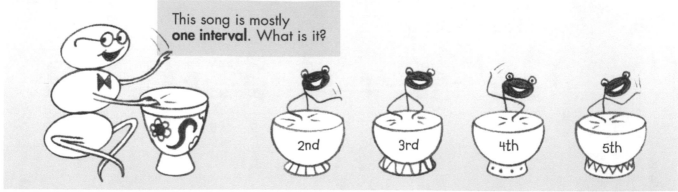

This song is mostly **one interval**. What is it?

DAY 4: Forest Drums

DON'T PRACTICE THIS!

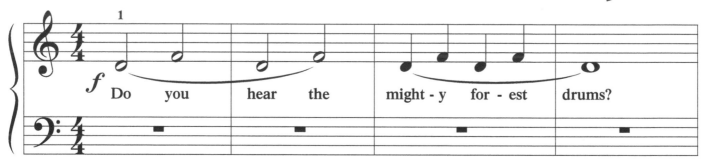

Do you hear the might-y for-est drums?

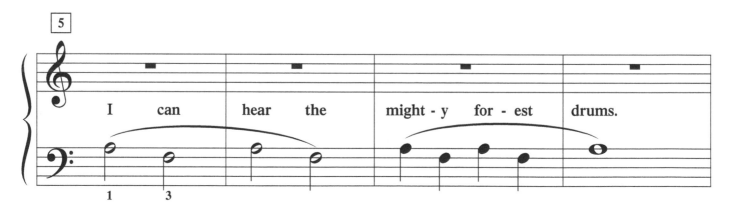

I can hear the might-y for-est drums.

Far a-way, far a-way, we can hear them call.

SIGHTREADING

DAY 5: Forest Drums

DON'T PRACTICE THIS!

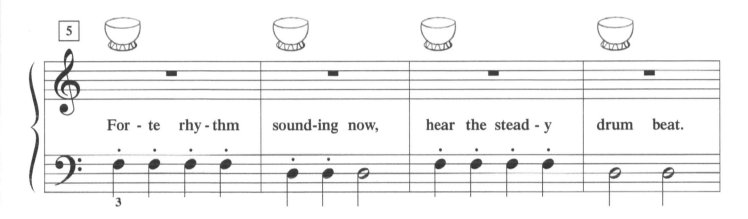

f Lis - ten to the for - est drums. Lis - ten to the drum beat.

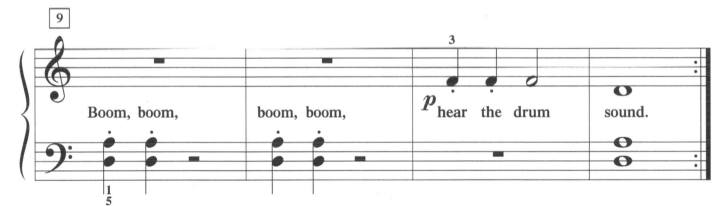

For - te rhy - thm sound-ing now, hear the stead - y drum beat.

Boom, boom, boom, boom, *p* hear the drum sound.

Write the **note names** in the drums above.

DAY 5! We're drumming for YOU!

DAY 1: Grumpy Old Troll

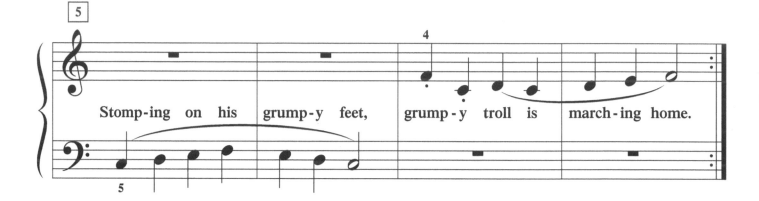

DAY 2: Grumpy Old Troll

DON'T PRACTICE THIS!

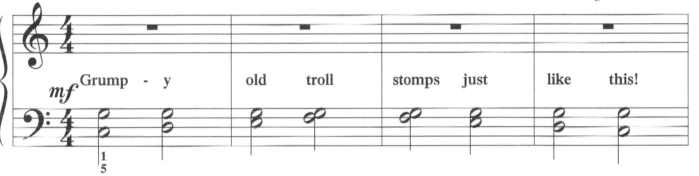

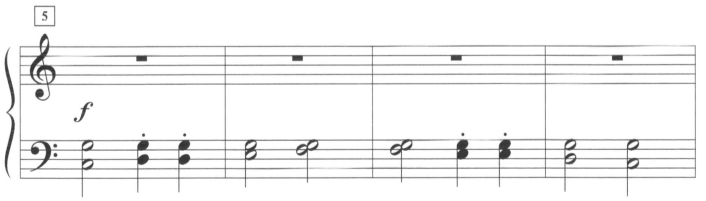

DAY 3: Grumpy Old Troll

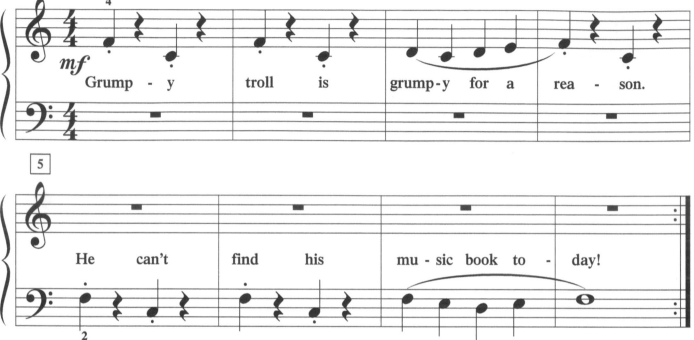

DAY 4: Grumpy Old Troll

DAY 5: Grumpy Old Troll

Use only finger 2's to play.

DON'T PRACTICE THIS!

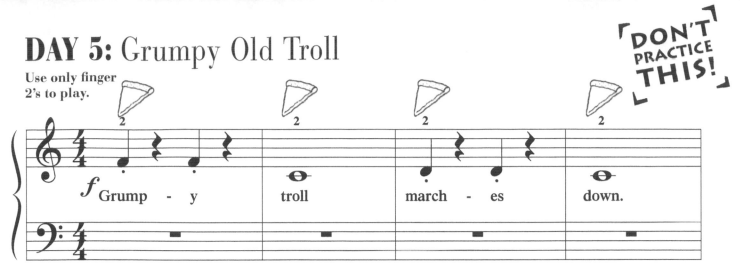

f Grump - y | troll | march - es | down.

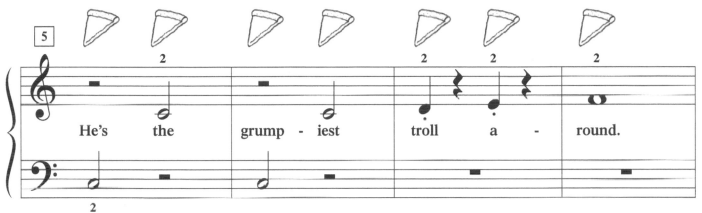

5 He's the | grump - iest | troll a - | round.

2

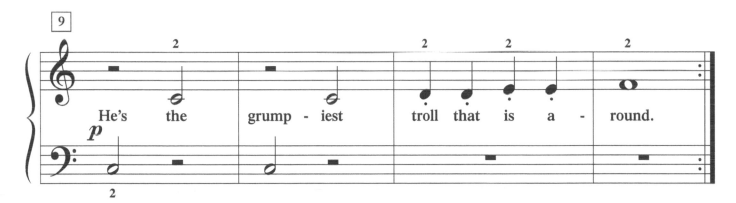

9 He's the | grump - iest | troll that is a - | round.

p

2

WRITE THE NOTE NAMES IN EACH PIZZA SLICE ABOVE.

Sightreader, I'm going to ignore you and eat my pizza. Pepperoni, yum! Cheese, yum! More, more, MORE!

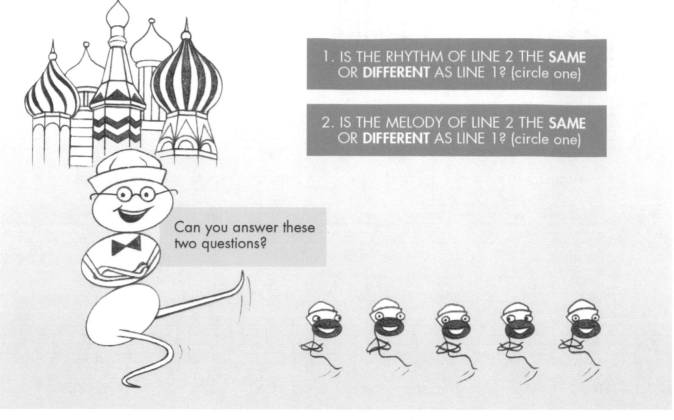

1. IS THE RHYTHM OF LINE 2 THE **SAME** OR **DIFFERENT** AS LINE 1? (circle one)

2. IS THE MELODY OF LINE 2 THE **SAME** OR **DIFFERENT** AS LINE 1? (circle one)

Can you answer these two questions?

DAY 1: Russian Sailor Dance

┌ DON'T PRACTICE **THIS!** ┐

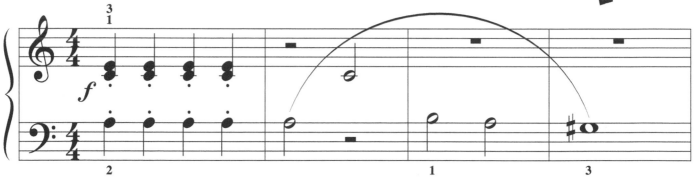

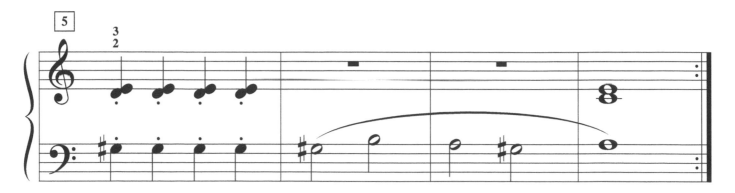

DAY 2: Russian Sailor Dance

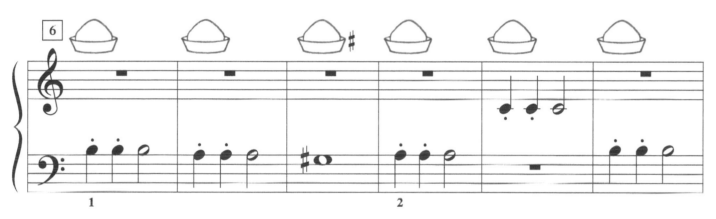

DAY 3: Russian Sailor Dance

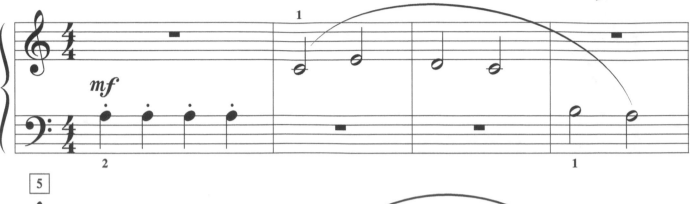

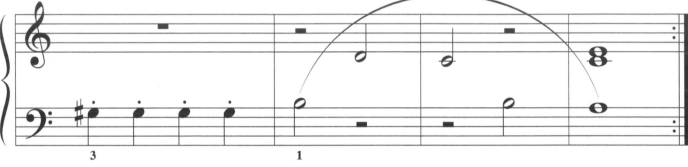

DAY 4: Russian Sailor Dance

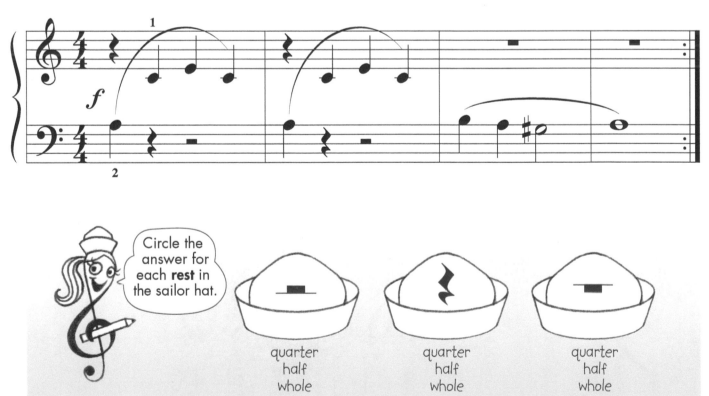

Circle the answer for each **rest** in the sailor hat.

quarter
half
whole

quarter
half
whole

quarter
half
whole

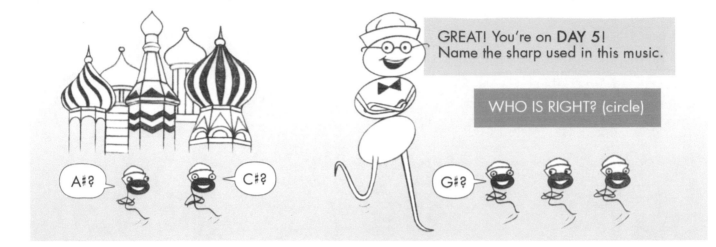

DAY 5: Russian Sailor Dance

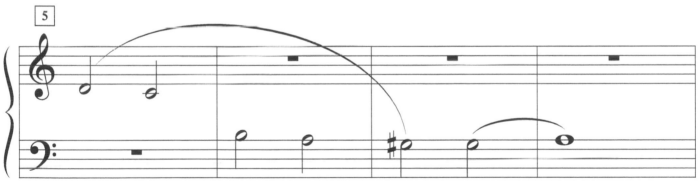

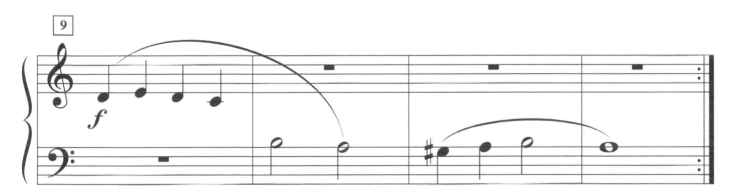

Circle the balloon that matches the **flat** in DAY 1.

DAY 1: Party Song

DON'T PRACTICE THIS!

Notice the L.H. fingering.

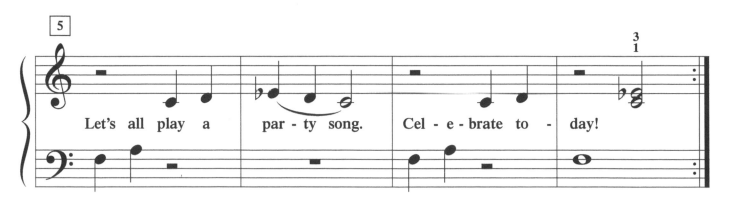

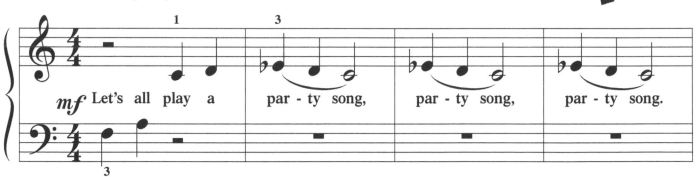

SIGHTREADING

DAY 2: Party Song

DON'T PRACTICE THIS!

Write the **note names** in the party hats above!

DAY 3: Party Song

DAY 4: Party Song

Notice the L.H. fingering.

SIGHTREADING

DAY 5: Party Song

Notice the L.H. fingering.

DON'T
PRACTICE
THIS!

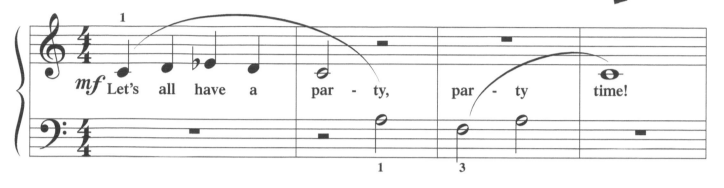

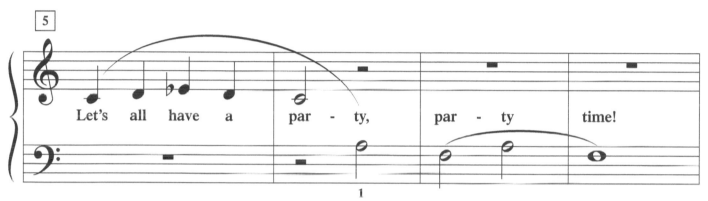

GOOD WORK, Sightreader!

You've come so far in the book!

Cheese flavor! YUM!

DAY 1: Song for a Scarecrow

DON'T PRACTICE THIS!

Is the first note Middle C or Treble C?

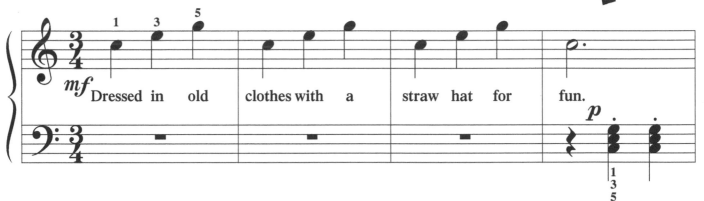

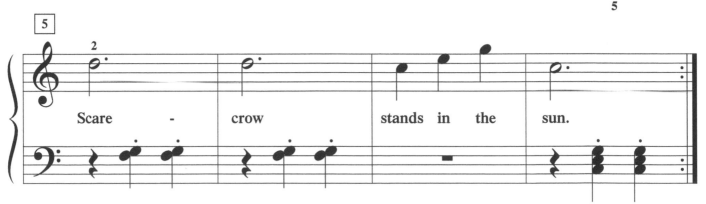

DAY 2: Song for a Scarecrow

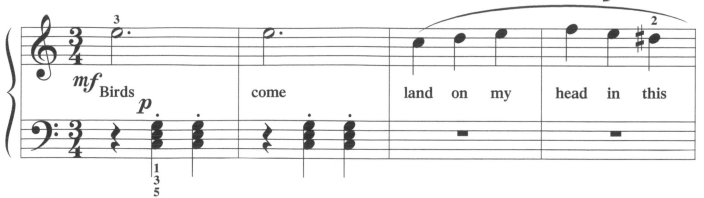

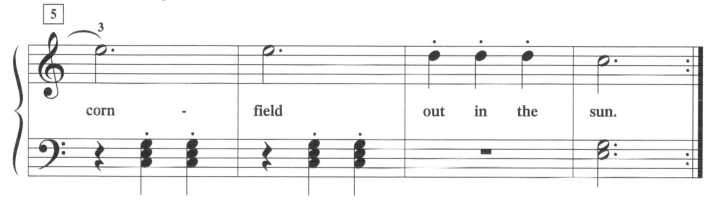

DAY 3: Song for a Scarecrow

DAY 4: Song for a Scarecrow

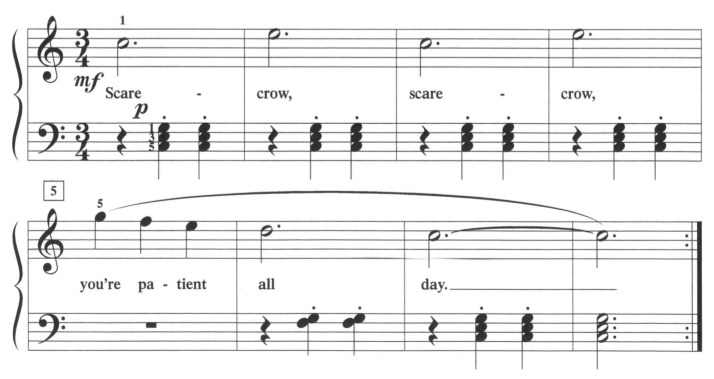

DAY 5: Song for a Scarecrow

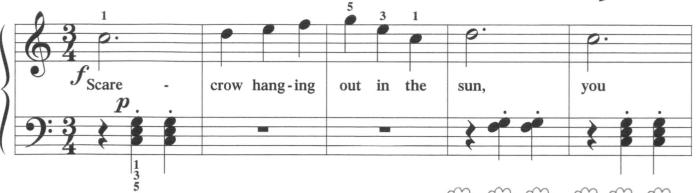

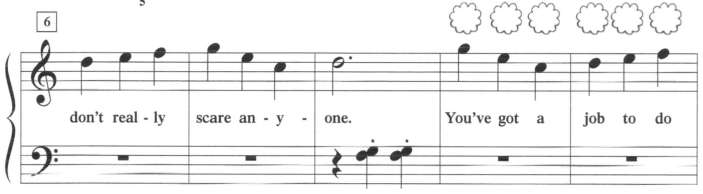

DAY 1: My Pony

DON'T PRACTICE THIS!

Neigh,   neigh,   neigh!   Po - ny, here's some hay.

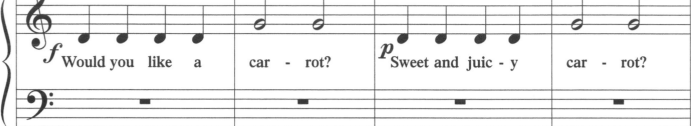

Would you   like   a   car - rot?   Sweet and juic - y   car - rot?

Neigh,   neigh,   neigh!   Po - ny, here's some hay.

I'm the teacher! Which line of music uses a **4th**?

Line 1.

Line 2.

WHO IS RIGHT? (circle)

Circle the apple with the **correct interval** for the measures below.

DAY 2: My Pony

DON'T PRACTICE THIS!

DAY 3: My Pony

DAY 4: My Pony

DAY 5: My Pony

DAY 1: London Symphony Theme

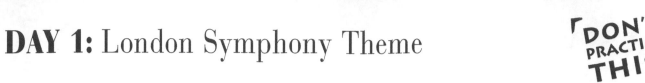

DAY 2: London Symphony Theme

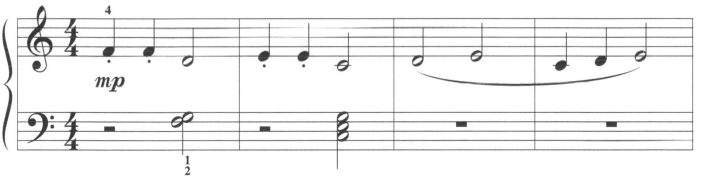

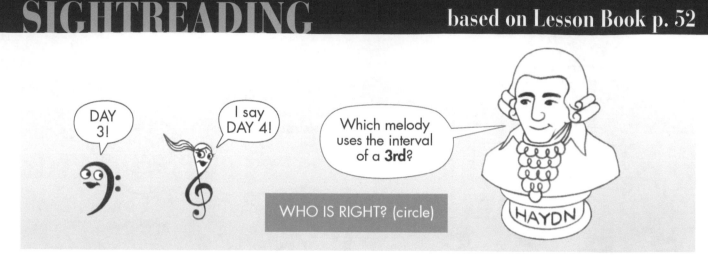

DAY 3: London Symphony Theme

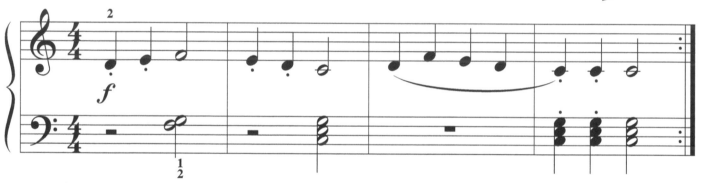

DAY 4: London Symphony Theme

DAY 5: London Symphony Theme

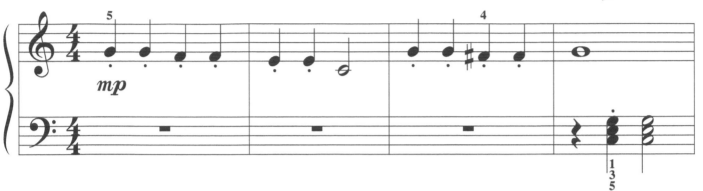

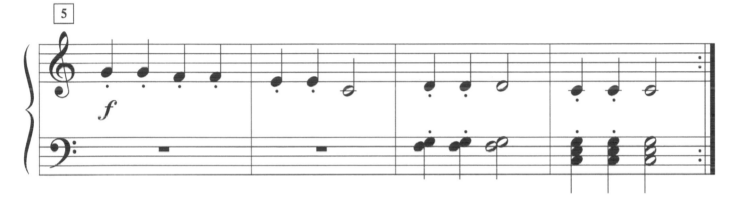

Ex. D#

DAY 1: Shepherd's Song

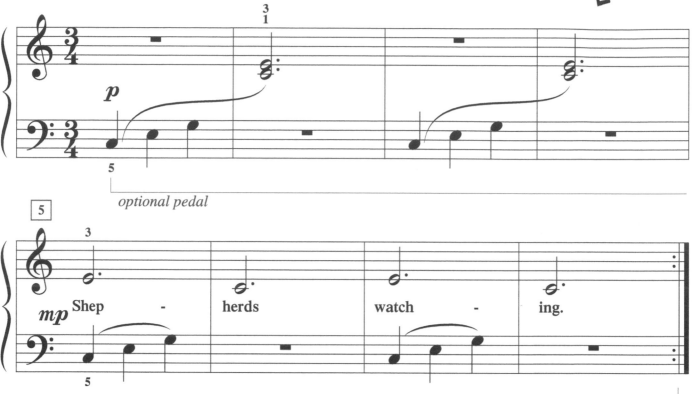

DAY 4: Shepherd's Song

Sunset is here.

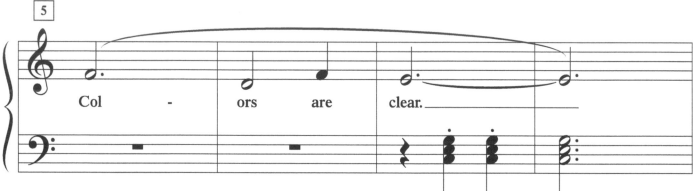

Colors are clear.

Red, orange, yellow,

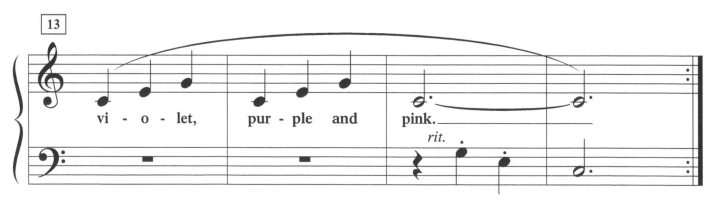

violet, purple and pink.

rit.

DAY 5: Shepherd's Song

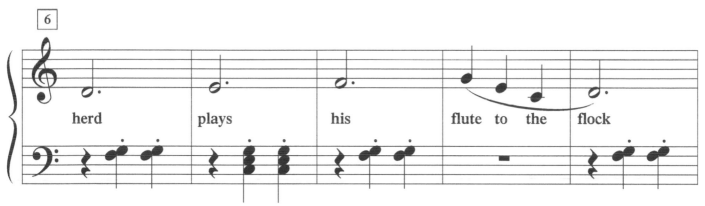

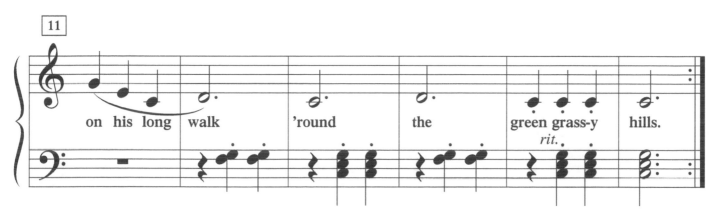

Name the **notes** of the dinosaur's roar!

He's really loud, and really cool!

DAY 1: Dinosaur Stomp

DON'T PRACTICE THIS!

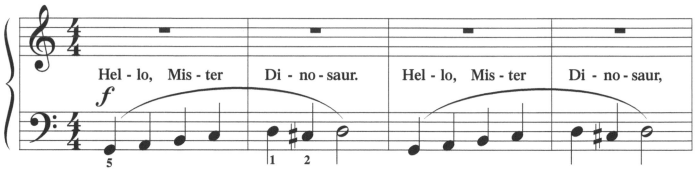

Hel - lo,   Mis - ter   Di - no - saur.   Hel - lo,   Mis - ter   Di - no - saur,

𝆑

5   1   2

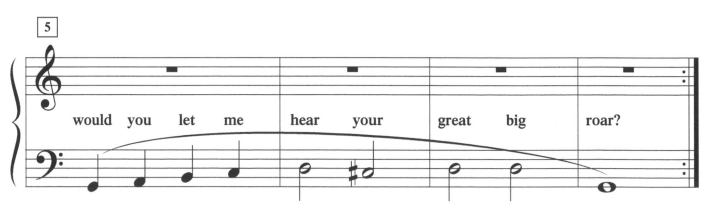

would   you   let   me   hear   your   great   big   roar?

DAY 2: Dinosaur Stomp

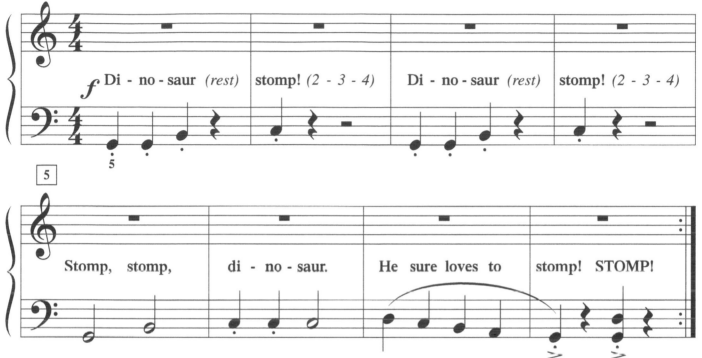

DAY 3: Dinosaur Stomp

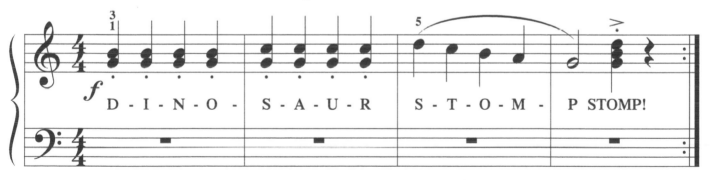

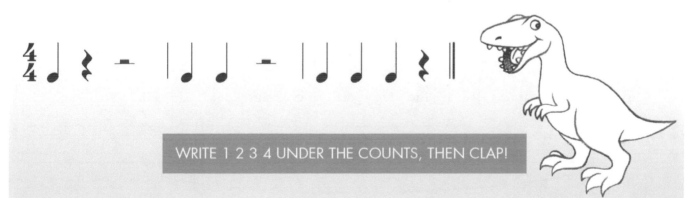

WRITE 1 2 3 4 UNDER THE COUNTS, THEN CLAP!

DAY 4: Dinosaur Stomp

DON'T
PRACTICE
THIS!

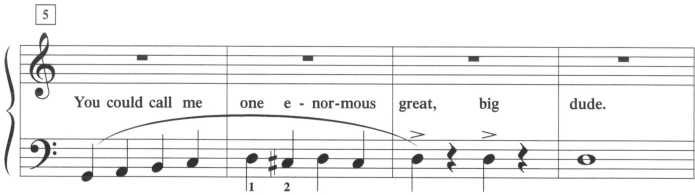

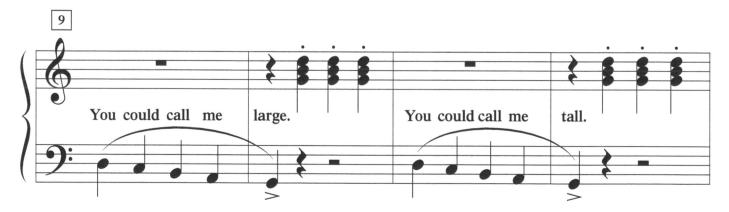

DAY 5: Dinosaur Stomp

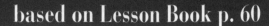

DAY 1: The Bubble

DAY 2: The Bubble

On which count does each **upbeat** begin?

count ___

count ___

count ___

count ___

DAY 3: The Bubble

DON'T PRACTICE THIS!

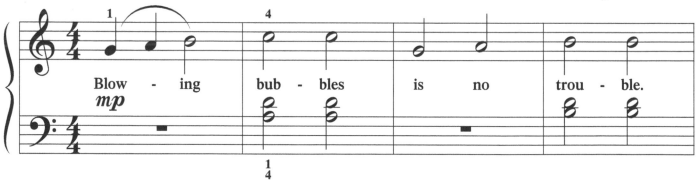

Blow - ing bub - bles is no trou - ble.
mp

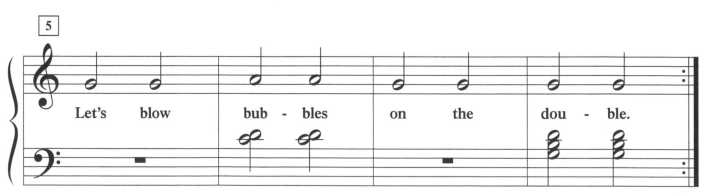

Let's blow bub - bles on the dou - ble.

SIGHTREADING

DAY 4: The Bubble

DON'T PRACTICE THIS!

Would you chew bub-ble gum in these fla-vors just for fun?

mf

Pep-per-mint or cher-ry twist? Pur-ple grape or how 'bout this?

f

Lem-on tang or or-ange blast, choc-'late gum that's made to last.

p

Tell me, what's your fa-v'rite one and write it just be-low for fun!

mf

(your favorite flavor)

DAY 5: The Bubble

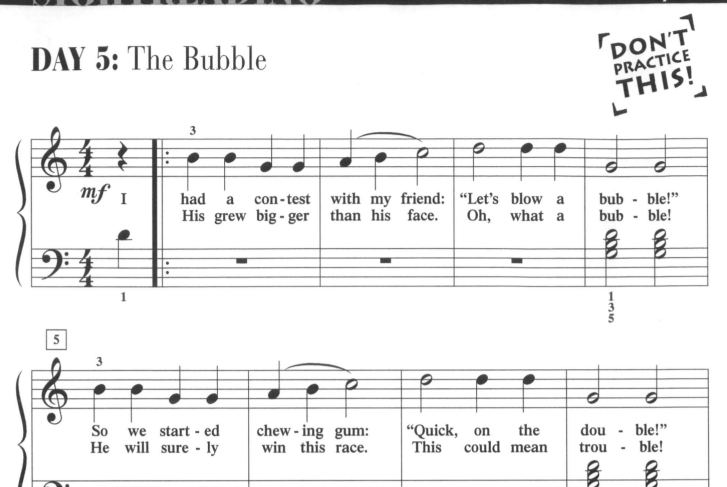

Piano Adventures® Certificate
CONGRATULATIONS

_____
(Your Name)

You are now a Level 1 Sightreader. Keep up the great work!

_____
Teacher

_____
Date

MOZART   HAYDN   BEETHOVEN